what men really think about

men's most frequent thoughts, ranked 1 to 100

Dr. Willie B. Hayve

mad moose press

Managing Editors: Simon Melhuish and Emma Craven
Series Editors: Simon Melhuish, Emma Craven,
Lee Linford and Nikole G Bamford
Cover Design: Alan Shiner

Designed and compiled by
Mad Moose Press
for
Lagoon Books
PO Box 311, KT2 5QW, UK
PO Box 990676, Boston, MA 02199, USA

ISBN: 1-904139-11-6

© MAD MOOSE PRESS 2001
Mad Moose Press and Lagoon Books are trade marks of
Lagoon Trading Company Limited.
All rights reserved.

No part of this publication may be reproduced, stored in a retrieval system, or transmitted in any form or by any other means electronic, mechanical, photocopying or otherwise, without prior permission in writing from the publisher.

www.madmoosepress.com
www.lagoongames.com

Printed in China.

TOP 100 THOUGHTS

what men really think about

men's most frequent thoughts, ranked 1 to 100

Dr. Willie B. Hayve

① SEX

2

SEX

3

SEX

4

SEX

5

SEX

⑥ SEX

7

SEX

8

SEX

9

SEX

10

SEX

11

SEX

12

SPORT

13
SEX

14
SEX

15

SEX

16

SEX

17

SEX

18

SEX

⑲ SEX

20

SEX

21

SEX

22

SEX

23

SEX

24

SEX

25

BEER

26
SEX

27
SEX

28

SEX

29

SEX

30

SEX

31

SEX

32

SEX

33

SEX

34

SEX

35

SEX

36

SEX

37

SEX

38

CARS

39
SEX

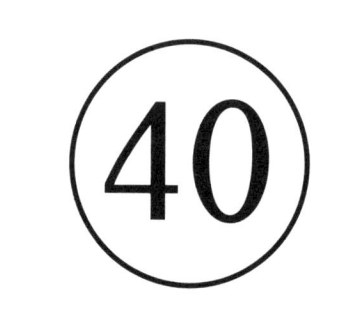

40
SEX

41

SEX

42

SEX

43

SEX

44

SEX

45

SEX

46

SEX

㊼

SEX

48

SEX

49

SEX

50

SEX

51

SEX

52

SPORT

53
SEX

54
SEX

55

SEX

56

SEX

ⓐ 57

SEX

58

SEX

59

SEX

60

SEX

61

SEX

62

SEX

63

SEX

64

SEX

65

SEX

66

BEER

67
SEX

68
SEX

69

SEX

70

SEX

71

SEX

72

SEX

73

SEX

74

SEX

75

SEX

76

SEX

… (77)

SEX

78

SEX

79

SEX

80

SPORT

⑧1

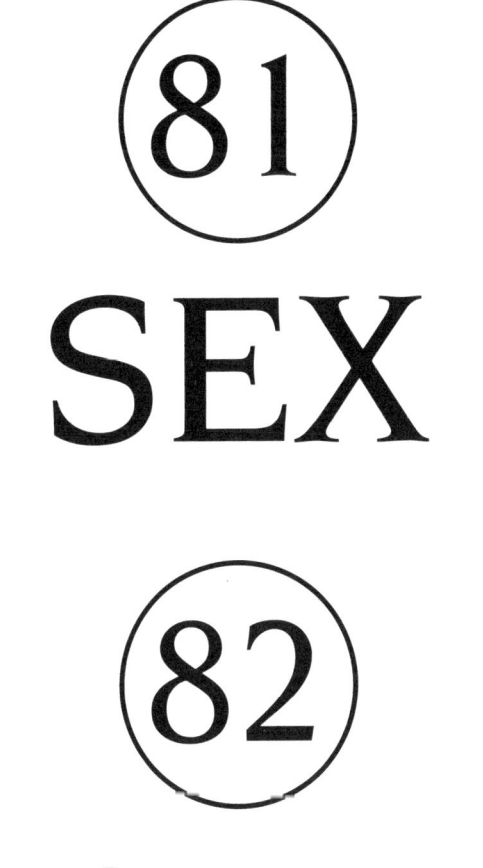

SEX

⑧2

SEX

83

SEX

84

SEX

85

SEX

86

SEX

(87) SEX

88

SEX

89

SEX

90

SEX

91

SEX

92

BEER

93
SEX

94
SEX

95

SEX

96

SEX

97

SEX

98

SEX

99

SEX

ⓘ00

SEX